The Breach

Naomi Wallace's plays include *In the Heart of America* (Bush Theatre), *Slaughter City* (Royal Shakespeare Company), *One Flea Spare* (Public Theater, New York City), *The Trestle at Pope Lick Creek* and *Things of Dry Hours* (New York Theatre Workshop), *The Fever Chart: Three Visions of the Middle East* (Public Lab, New York City), *And I and Silence* (Finborough Theatre, London, and Signature Theatre, NYC), *Night is a Room* (Signature Theatre, NYC) and, with Ismail Khalidi, adapted from the novella by Ghassan Kanafani, *Returning to Haifa* (Finborough Theatre, London.) Her work has received numerous awards including the Obie Award, the Horton Foote Award and a MacArthur Fellowship. In 2013, she received the inaugural Windham-Campbell Prize for Drama, and in 2015 an Arts and Letters Award in Literature. Her play *One Flea Spare* is in the permanent repertoire of the French National Theatre, the Comédie-Française.

T0323170

also by Naomi Wallace from Faber

THE BREACH

Note

This story happens in 1977 and 1991,
in the basement of a white, working-class household.

The set should be minimal and not naturalistic.

The couch isn't really there.

There is nothing on the porch so the older characters
always stand.

The wilder the moment, the more still the body.

No one cries in this story.

'I'll look back at today,
at the placid lake where
you're sailing away.

I'll conjugate: I lost,
you lost, we lost.
The we that was is wind.'

Andrea Cohen, 'Past Participle'

'No more can I be sever'd from your side
Than can yourself yourself in twain divide.'

William Shakespeare, *Henry VI, Part i*

NAOMI WALLACE

The Breach

faber

First published in 2022
by Faber and Faber Limited
74–77 Great Russell Street, London WC1B 3DA

Typeset by Brighton Gray
Printed and bound in the UK by CPI Group (Ltd), Croydon CR0 4YY

The right of Naomi Wallace to be identified as author
of this work has been asserted in accordance with Section 77
of the Copyright, Designs and Patents Act 1988

With thanks to Andrea Cohen for permission to quote 'Past Participle'

A CIP record for this book
is available from the British Library

ISBN 978-0-571-37922-4

2 4 6 8 10 9 7 5 3 1

The Breach was first performed at Hampstead Theatre, London, on 6 May 2022. The cast was as follows:

Frayne (1977) Charlie Beck
Jude (1991) Jasmine Blackborow
Hoke (1977) Alfie Jones
Hoke (1991) Tom Lewis
Frayne (1991) Douggie McMeekin
Acton (1977) Stanley Morgan
Jude (1977) Shannon Tarbet

Director Sarah Frankcom
Designer Naomi Dawson
Lighting Rick Fisher
Sound Tingying Dong
Movement Jennifer Jackson
Voice Michaela Kennen
Projection Content Timothy Kelly
Casting Nadine Rennie CDG
Assistant Director Tramaine Reindorf

This play is for Sarah Burke

Characters

Setting

The Diggs' basement, and the Diggs' porch.

*The play takes place somewhere just outside a
half-remembered city in Kentucky.*

Act One

The Diggs' basement. 1977. End August. Sparse, worn, clean.

Lights up on an almost seventeen-year-old Jude. A smart, confident beauty in colorful patched blue jeans and a tank top. She is holding two screwdrivers out at arm's length, one each pointing at Hoke and Frayne's chest. Hoke is more fearful than Frayne. Frayne carries a basketball under his arm which he hardly ever bounces.

Jude You ever heard it? Nah. Well I have. On Tucker's farm. Wet, pathetic and exactly like this idiot's voice: the fart of a cow.

Jude moves a little closer with her screwdrivers.

It's a shit little song, right?

Hoke *and* **Frayne** Right.

Frayne Crap.

Hoke Bingo. Absolutely.

Jude Then who brought that single into our home?

Hoke *and* **Frayne** Hoke did! Frayne did!

Hoke Most girls are fans so I /

Jude I'm not most girls.

Frayne Say that again.

Jude Boys. I got a radio upstairs that sounds like the Little Train that Won't Ever Again. Now my mom loves to listen to that radio when she gets home from work, so I'm gonna make the sweetheart sing again if I have to tear out its guts

5

and feed them backwards through the dials. But I can't concentrate when you put on that record and I got to come down here and shut it off.

Hoke *and* **Frayne** Sorry. / Won't happen again. / Never again.

Jude lowers the screwdrivers.

Jude (*to Hoke*) I seen you on the bench last spring. Poke?

Hoke Hoke.

Jude Coach never lets you play.

Hoke Quarterback. This season I'll play quarterback.

Jude So you're an up and coming, huh? Cheerleaders are gonna eat your pretty face.

Hoke I'll bring the salt and pepper.

Jude Sing it, then. If you love it so much.

Hoke My living room is the size of your house. Entirely.

Jude Well that explains your taste in music.

Hoke You know what? There's a brand spankin' Firebird parked in your drive this very minute. Got it for my sixteenth. And the tank's full.

Frayne Tank's always full.

Hoke Where do you want to go?

Jude puts the screwdriver close to Hoke's throat.

Jude Sing the song, guttersnipe, or I'll dent you.

Frayne Better do what she says, Hoke.

Hoke nervously sings the David Cassidy song 'Rock Me Baby'.

Jude Sing the chorus. That's the best worst part.

Hoke gathers himself, and sings it ('Euwwwww, rock me, baby'), then suddenly snatches the screwdriver from Jude and uses it as a microphone, like a pop star. After singing another verse, he plays air guitar for a few moments, but then breaks off abruptly, suddenly embarrassed. He hands the screwdriver back to Jude.

My brother is thirteen years old. He's still a kid.

Hoke A bright kid.

Frayne Almost fourteen.

Jude And he's been writing your essays for summer make-up classes.

Hoke And he's sworn to get me through SATs this fall, in science and math.

Frayne Promised to scribble up some lyricals on Dickenshit for me this semester.

Jude (*to Hoke*) But neither of you offered to pay him.
(*To Frayne.*) It's Dickinson in this house, and she would've spent your dime, kid.

Hoke Money doesn't matter to us.

Jude How many boys are in this . . . club?

Hoke Frayne and myself. Acton is gonna join us. It'll be exclusive. Just the three of us.

Frayne We're like this.

Frayne shows crossed fingers.

Hoke And when we go to college –

Jude If.

Hoke Your brother sticks with me and it's 'when'.

Jude He'll make his own way if he gets a scholarship.

Hoke He won't need one. I've got strings.

Jude Huh. What kind of strings?

Hoke Confidential ones. The good strings always are. My dad, his two best buddies from way back in grade school work in his office. They didn't even need to go to college 'cause my dad pulled –

Hoke *and* **Jude** Some strings.

Hoke Exactly. What's a guttersnipe?

Jude My brother doesn't need to join your club.

Hoke Maybe not. But in a few years he'll need my strings.

Frayne He needs 'em now, so no one'll ever drag him in the storage room at school again, strip him, pour glue all over his skinny body and shower him with confetti.

Acton appears with a small paper bag. They others don't yet see him.

Hoke Couldn't believe it when I saw him running half naked through lunch hall, like some kind of crazy Christmas ornament. We laughed so hard a window broke.

Acton (*appearing, facts*) Window broke 'cause I hit it with my elbow when I slipped on some chilli beans a kid threw at me as I ran by.
    (*To Jude.*) Judith. I already joined the club, weeks ago.

Jude What? No. Acton.

Acton says the following all in one breath, though it's not rushed.

Acton Know what it feels like to tap on up to the same kids that used to pinch me, kick me, hawk on me, and now get so close up in their face I'm spitting on them as I talk and they don't dare wipe it off and I can say 'cock-a-doodle doo' or 'gumbo, bumbo, ass-a-wacky trumbo' and jab their cheek with my finger and they nod like they know what I'm talking about and they don't disagree or move an inch 'cause Hoke and Frayne, my new brothers, are rising up behind me like floodlights and these punks know, they know that if they ever touch one hair on my head again, they'll be taken out back and kicked into the size of a football.

Acton uses his inhaler.

Hoke (*speaks the line*) 'Rock me, baby.'

Frayne Damn right.

Jude (*to Hoke*) So you know how to keep my brother safe?

Hoke That's Frayne's job.

Frayne I say 'How hard?' 'fore Hoke says 'Hit 'im'.

Jude (*to Acton*) Acton. These two are stone-cold cheese weasels /

Acton They're my friends.

Acton hands Frayne the paper bag. Its a pint of whiskey.

And my shields. Something you can't be, Jude.

Frayne drinks.

Frayne We're taking good care of him.

Hoke drinks.

Hoke Promise. Your mom ever come down here?

Acton Not if we keep it clean.

Hoke You two should move to the 'burbs. This is howdie-doodie land out here.

Frayne Yeah, and I can't believe our Prom Queen pulled a tool on us. I like it.

Jude I can hit an apple with a knife from thirty feet and it'll stick.

Acton She can. Dad taught her. He tried to teach me too but my hands shake on account of my asthma.

Acton holds out his hand to show them.

Hoke Acton. We're gonna take the shake out of your bake.

Frayne The yank out of your crank. How'd you get the whiskey when you got no ID?

Acton A handwritten note from my mom's doctor who has proscribed JD for her arthritis.

Frayne Your mom's prescription?

Jude Mom doesn't drink.

Acton Thats why I wrote it myself.

Hoke Smart as a tack.

Acton I gave the man a tip so he'll remember me.

Hoke Good business sense too.

Hoke hands the bottle to Acton. Jude snatches it away.

Jude He's too young to drink.

Acton Judith . . .

Jude takes a drink herself. Then relents and gives Acton the bottle.

Jude Just a sip. It's not Orange Crush.

Acton gasps after swallowing. Hoke takes the bottle and pockets it.

Hoke This place could be our headquarters.

Acton Yeah. It could!

Jude No way in hell.

Frayne Cozy down here. Private.

Hoke Though it's small. Small.

Jude So are my tits.

Hoke doesn't know how to answer.

Frayne More than a mouthful's a waste, I heard it said.

Jude (*nods 'thanks' to Frayne*) That's right, and how old are you, fourteen?

Frayne Sixteen. In a few. Frayne. Glad to meet you. Though I seen you in the hall for years now.

Frayne holds out his hand but Jude ignores it.

Jude Mr Frayne, sixteen-in-a-few whom I've not noticed before, bet you never sucked a girl's tit.

Acton Oh no . . .

Hoke Jesus, what a mouth.

Jude Well?

Frayne Define suck.

Acton Don't.

Jude gives her forefinger a practical suck.

Frayne Not sucked, no. But I had what I'd call a.

Jude A what?

Hoke What?

Frayne A slurp.

Jude A slurp? How's that go?

Frayne Well it's a kind of drive-by suck; only lasts a second.

Jude (*to Hoke*) And you? Poke.

Acton His name is *Hoke.*

Hoke Do I look like a slurper to you? Not me. I've. *Imbibed* the nipple while I fingered the goose. Last June, after the Prom dance.

Frayne You never told me! Who'd you finger?

Hoke Chrissy.

Jude *and* **Frayne** Chrissy who?

Hoke She fell asleep after a few drinks at my place. I peeped her shirt up, then her bra and latched on.

Acton Keep going.

Hoke Her nipples were rodeo and I /

Frayne Chrissy Brennan?

Hoke Then I slipped my fingers under her skirt /

Jude Chrissy Jeds?

Hoke Wrote my name on her windowpane.

Frayne (*thinks he's got it*) Chrissy Moreland!

Hoke No, damn it. Chrissy my aunt!

All Jesus. Shit. Your aunt? That's wrong. Disgusting.

Hoke She's only thirty-four.

Frayne That's incest, bud.

Hoke I thought so too at first but then I figured since she was out cold she never knew it happened so in a way it didn't and the next time I saw Aunt Chrissy she bought me a Coke and ruffled my hair like a puppy. No harm done.

Jude So I'm surrounded by slurping, perverted virgins.

Hoke *and* **Frayne** (*lying*) I'm not a virgin!

Acton I am.

Frayne The more interesting question's got to be: is the Prom Queen a virgin? I hear. Not.

Hoke I bet: not.

Jude Won't tell you twerps nothin'.

Hoke Come on.

Jude 'Cause I'm not in your 'club'.

Frayne We told you.

Acton They can keep a secret, Jude. You can trust them.

Jude (*considers*) I'm seventeen in a couple of months. Most of my girlfriends have had two or three. Me. I've had.

Jude pauses, playing with them. Hoke and Frayne lean in; suspense.

Two. (*Beat.*) And a half.

Hoke And a half?

Frayne What the hell?

Hoke You mean he couldn't get it up?

Jude Couldn't get an . . . 'erection'?

Acton Please don't say that word, Jude.

Jude That wasn't it. I mean it was an inch long when hard.

Frayne Damn.

Hoke Poor guy.

Jude Yep. That big.

Jude demonstrates with her fingers.

Like a Gerber weenie. Until I saw it I never would've believed God made 'em that short. And he was six foot. Sweet guy too.

Hoke *and* **Frayne** Who?

Jude Out-of-towner. Orlando, last winter. Met him at –

Acton – the Wet and Wild Aquatic Theme Park?! That Richard guy?!

Jude That Richard guy.

Acton I did a backflip off his shoulders.

Jude Richard knew how to use his tongue.

Acton He bought me a hot dog.

Frayne She's a dirty girl, your big sis.

Jude (*facts*) But she's not a slut.

Frayne I like it.

Jude You got to do six or seven to qualify for slut.

Frayne Pretty and pretty smart.

Jude Save it, jailbait. You're fifteen, remember?

Acton (*to Hoke*) Can we take your Firebird up to the Convenient? I wanna get a shake.

Hoke Yep.

Jude I got to be at work at seven.

Hoke Let me give you a ride to work.

Frayne Why don't we let Acton drive?

Hoke Sure again.

Jude No fuckin' way.

Acton I don't know how to drive.

Hoke and Frayne recount the following story together, with ease, having fun.

Frayne Hoke'll teach you. Me, I take my brother's Pacer out when my folks are asleep. Two weeks ago a cop pulls me over and asks for my driver's license. I shrug and say:

Hoke 'I'm fifteen.'

Frayne He says:

Hoke 'Get out of the car, son.'

Frayne I say, what I usually say in those circumstances:

Hoke 'But Mister, my brother Terry's got shrapnel in his back from Vietnam and he can't walk anymore so when he moves even the tiniest bit . . .'

Frayne '. . . he screams like a roller coaster.'

Hoke makes the scream of a roller coaster.

Yeah. Just like that. 'Officer, my brother can't sleep at night so I had to take his car to get him some aspirin 'cause he needs to chomp a bottle a night to keep the war noise down.'

Hoke Terry used to laugh all the time. Irritated the hell out of us.

Frayne We called him Jello, always –

Hoke – jigglin'. But now he doesn't laugh.

Frayne Now he gurgles. I guess you could say that gurgling is a kind of laugh.

Jude I saw your brother Terry once, with your folks at a football game. He's handsome.

Frayne Yeah. He is. But he won't ever slurp no tit.

Jude I'm sorry about your brother.

Frayne Sure you are. About as sorry as I am about your dad. And that's not much, right?

Silence a moment. Then Jude moves to whack Frayne but instead she suddenly gives him a quick kiss on the mouth. He's stunned.

Acton Jude!

Hoke Hey! Why'd you kiss him?

Jude (*facts*) I didn't kiss him.

Hoke Yes you did!

Acton Stop it, Frayne.

Hoke Why'd you kiss Frayne?

Frayne (*to Acton*) Hey. *She* kissed *me*.

Acton Well don't kiss her back! If you're my brother now, then she's your sister too. Don't kiss your sister.

Frayne I didn't kiss her. *She* kissed *me*.

Jude Liar. You couldn't pay me to kiss you. You're pathetic.

Jude kisses Frayne again.

Hoke What the fuck? Why's he getting all the abuse? I'm the lost kid here. An only kid too, besides my sister. And my house is so big I need track shoes to get from room to room. My dad smells like the inside of a briefcase. My mom *is* the inside of a briefcase 'cause she's the brains of the business and my favorite rocker is David Cassidy. Can you get any more pathetic than that?

Acton (*sincerely*) He's got a point, Jude. Maybe you should kiss Hoke too.

Jude You think so?

Acton Just to be fair.

Jude considers. She moves a little closer to Hoke. He's nervous but holds his ground. Jude kisses him.

Hoke (*sincerely*) Is it. Was it gross? How do I taste?

Jude Well. You taste kind of (*Beat.*) stupid.

Hoke is crestfallen.

Acton What's stupid taste like?

Jude (*shrugs*) Kinda. Sweet . . .? Listen up. This is our home.
(*To Hoke and Frayne.*) Not yours. Not yours. And I'm the head of this household.

Acton She is.

Acton picks up his guitar and strums a few notes as background to Jude's proclamation.

Jude I work nights and weekends and I pay half the bills.

Frayne 'Cause your mom got fired.

Jude She didn't get fired.

Hoke That's what we heard.

Jude She's on strike! There's a difference.
Learn it or I'll hit you. I can reach my arm, up to the elbow, down the kitchen drainpipe –

Acton She can.

Jude – and grab a hairball by its greasy fuckin' neck and yank it out. I can lift my mom out of the bath when she's too tired to do it herself. I'm the best looking girl in high school, not counting Sarah Burke, but she's my best friend so I don't care. I cut and sew most of our clothes. I eat like a horse.

Acton She does.

Jude And my turds stretch from here to the end of the street, that long.

Acton Unfortunately, true.

Jude So if you're thinking of using this basement as your headquarters, think again or die.

Hoke I like this basement. I'll give you five bucks a week for it if we get free rein.

Jude No way.

Hoke How about seven.

Jude Fifteen or nothing.

Hoke Eight. It's stagflation, remember?

Jude calmly shakes her head 'no'.

Frayne (*to Hoke*) I'm not paying her nothin'. Let's go somewhere else.

Acton Come on, Jude. Eight is a lot!

Jude Nope.

Hoke Okay. Ten bucks a week.

Acton Wow.

Frayne Christ.

Hoke But we come and go as we please and you keep your mom out of here.

Jude takes a moment to consider, then she and Hoke shake on it.

Jude Deal. But whatever you do down here: Do. Not. Mess. With.

Jude *and* **Acton** My kingdom.

Jude Agreed?

Hoke *and* **Frayne** Agreed.

Jude (*interrupts Acton's strumming*) Play me my song. I'm feelin' stoked.

Acton I'm sick of that song.

Jude Come on. Play it. I need it.

Acton is reluctant, but then suddenly bounces into the lively intro chords of Eric Clapton's 'Layla'. Jude begins to dance. Hoke and Frayne are mesmerized. Then Acton puts down his guitar, though the music/song continues and becomes the real version of the song. Darkness. Jude continues to dance alone in the dark.

SCENE TWO

Fourteen years later, in the Diggs' basement. 1991. October. It's almost the same basement, but unused.

Young Jude continues to dance, unseen, in darkness, then without music.

When Hoke, Frayne and Jude appear Young Jude leaves; they do not see her. The three of them are initially uncomfortable with one another, subdued.

Sudden bright light.

Hoke It even smells the same. Unbelievable.

Frayne Mold.

Jude Would either of you like a sandwich?

Hoke That's not mold. That's.
(*Breathes deep.*) That's – Whoa. Takes me back.

Jude Mayo and cheese okay?

Frayne How 'bout we go down the The Captain's Quarters, for old times' sake. Sit by the river?

Hoke Nah, they close the outdoor section mid October.

Jude I've got pretzels and peanuts left over. He didn't have a lot of friends, did he?

Hoke Sure. But shy types.

Jude All his friends are shy? Only three people came this afternoon. From his work, they said.

Frayne I don't know them. Though I seen that one skinny guy before.

Jude Hardly a memorial.

Hoke You said it wasn't a memorial. You said it was just a 'gathering of friends'.

Jude A gathering, yeah. How many make a gathering?

Frayne A handful, plus us?

Hoke looks around reverently.

Hoke This is. Damn. The same stuff? If you're not gonna take it with you, I'll give you a good deal on it. Including that old fridge and stove in the kitchen. They made 'em like tanks back then. Run forever.

Jude and Frayne just look at him.

Oh. We just bought a cabin up on Lake Cumberland and I haven't had the time to furnish the /

Jude (*straight*) Whose decision was it to burn my brother?

Frayne Cremate.

Hoke We couldn't locate you, Jude, so we decided on cremation.

Frayne We didn't even know if you were alive.

Jude How much did it cost?

Frayne Hoke took care of the bill.

Jude Then what do I owe you /

Hoke No way. I was happy to take care of it.

Jude Thank you.

Hoke just nods.

Frayne So how do you like. Uh.

Jude Austin.

Hoke Word is it's an up and coming city.

Jude Is it?

Hoke But then so is ours.

Frayne You thought of movin' back here?

Jude Can't. I got ties.

Hoke Someone special in Austin?

Jude I married when I was nineteen. But then we divorced.

Hoke I'm sorry.

Jude A book. A chair. A dog's bowl, smack across the face.

Frayne Damn.

Hoke The bastard.

Jude Those were the things I hit him with when my hands weren't hard enough. He wouldn't hit me back. Bastard is right.

Frayne If I had a wife, I'd give her what she wanted.

Hoke (*quietly*) Shut up, Frayne.

Frayne I'd hit her back.

Frayne pretends to box with Jude.

Still need to let it all out? Come on. Come on.

Jude smiles, nods her head 'no'.

Hoke It's good to see you, Jude.

Frayne quits boxing.

Frayne Yeah. It is.

Jude (*to Hoke*) And you? A boy and a girl, right?

Hoke Eight and ten years old.

Hoke gets out photos.

And I don't hit my wife, Carol. My beautiful wife, I might add.

Jude looks through the photos.

Jude Yes. She's beautiful.

Hoke And she doesn't want me to hit her either. Never cheated on Carol. Not once. That's Nickie. That's Annie.

Jude They're. Lovely.

Frayne They're ugly. I've seen 'em up close.

Hoke Fuck you, Frayne.

Frayne Carol's a looker. You're about average. So how does one beauty plus Joe Average equal two ugly kids?

Hoke (*to Jude*) It burns me up sometimes, 'cause I love them so much.

Frayne Their heads are too small.

Jude (*to Frayne*) You got kids?

Frayne Not yet.

Jude In the making?

Frayne Not yet. You?

Jude Yes. One. From a casual friend. No ties.

Hoke Boy or girl?

Jude Girl. Six years old. She's very tall, my Linda. So smart. She can take any number and turn it into a word.

Frayne What's that mean?

Jude Linda lives with friends of mine. Sometimes she hugs me so hard my ribs ache.

Hoke So you don't have her full time?

Jude Unfortunately, no. I get her on the weekends.

Hoke I could never do without my kids. No way. I need to see them every day, hear their voices /

Jude Well, there were some hard years when I was very.

Frayne Fucked up?

Jude Poor. I couldn't give her what she needed.

Hoke Kids just need love.

Jude I'm getting a better place to live this fall. Then me and Linda are gonna make up for lost time.

Hoke All these years –

Jude Fourteen. Years.

Hoke – at any time, you could've called on us. We'd've helped you out if you needed it. You know that, right?

Jude I know that.

Frayne One day you were here, the next day, gone.

Hoke Ran away to the Sunshine State.

Jude My grandmother was sick.

Hoke That's what we heard.

Jude Acton was too young to go, and Mom couldn't leave work.

Hoke Sounds like you've had some tough times. I could get you some medication for feeling like that.

Jude For feeling poor?

Hoke For feeling depressed.

Jude I've never been depressed.

Frayne I was on one of Hoke's prescriptions for a few years. Expensive, that shit.

Hoke Hey, I made your insurance company, which is mine, pay for all of it. We set you up with the best doc in the city. Rage, rage. Cry, cry –

Frayne – then a glass of water and a pea-sized pill –

Hoke – and hello, quiettttt.

Frayne Like an empty street at night.

Hoke Shoulda stayed on the meds, Frayne.

Frayne (*an old refrain*) I'd still be working for you if I had.

Hoke That's right. You'd still be making six pretty digits /

Frayne (*to Jude*) How come you didn't come back till now?

Jude I meant to.

Hoke Acton said you spoke on the phone sometimes.

Jude Did he? It wasn't easy for my family, we were just kids when my father /

Hoke We all know what happened, Jude. We all knew your family had it hard.

Jude Did you know about the scaffolding?

Hoke We sure did. Your father hit –

Frayne – every piece of it on his way down. Fire department had to use a crane to get his arm down. It was hanging on a cable on the ninth floor, waving at the city below.

Jude smiles at Frayne's honesty.

Jude His arm was not waving. He was giving the *Fuck You* to the bastards who let him fall.

Hoke A tragic accident.

Jude Yes, that was the ruling. But most of their halters were worn out. Company refused to replace them. I didn't know it was one of your father's construction sites till years later.

Hoke Neither did I but we all knew your mom got a payout.

Jude Just enough to pay the rent for a few months and take care of Dad's funeral. We sure were living it up back then.

Frayne Come on. We did have some good times.

Hoke Undoubtedly. Like your birthday party, outdoors. Whoa. It was huge.

Frayne Nine kegs. We set that field on fire.

Hoke Wild, wild horses.

Frayne You danced all night on Nash's pick-up. Put dents in his hood. Man, was Nash pissed.

Hoke There must've been over two hundred kids there that night and most of them loaded. You were a very popular girl, Jude. People still talk about that night.

Jude Do they?

Hoke Yeah. There wasn't a blade of grass left in that field after we finished with it. Just mud.

Frayne Cops broke it up at two a.m. Remember. They even used a 'copter.

Hoke (*to Jude*) And you, my friend, were totally toast-wasted.

Jude (*remembering*) Yeah I was. Mimi, Thea, Sarah carried me home. Had to prop me up so I wouldn't puke and choke.

Hoke Never hit a high like that night again, did we, Frayne?

Frayne There were a lot of wild parties back then.

Hoke Come on. Jude's seventeenth was *the* party of our youth and you know it. We didn't get home till four a.m. We stripped and ran circles in my front yard to see who could be the best chicken with its head cut off. Then we went inside and each had a bowl –

Frayne – of Captain Crunch, still naked –

Hoke – and my dad came down, joined us in his PJs, gave us a lesson about the sweet meats of accelerated –

Hoke *and* **Frayne** – deregulation!

Frayne Yeah. Don't remind me. And he asked us what he should name his –

Hoke – new health insurance company and we said:

Frayne Y-A-N-S-A-H. Yansah.

Hoke You Are Not Sick, Ass Hole.

Frayne Thatab. T-H-A-T-A-B.

Hoke That's Not A Tumor, That's A Bruise. My pops was building a hospital a month back then.

Frayne We had your dad rollin' on the floor laughin'.

Hoke R-I-A-L-W-C. He came up with Rial WC.

Frayne I don't remember that one.

Hoke Rigor Mortis Is A Left Wing Conspiracy. Oh what a night.

Jude Well, I don't remember most of it and it was my birthday.

Hoke The best days are the ones you don't remember.

Jude I wanted to see my brother's body.

Hoke Like we said, we couldn't reach any next of kin.

Jude How was he?

Frayne What do you mean?

Jude After our mother died.

Frayne I was at your mom's funeral.

Hoke (*to Jude*) And you weren't there for that one either. Four years ago. Five? I was out of town on business. A stroke, right?

Jude Right.

Hoke I sent a ring of flowers 'bout the size of a boat.

Frayne Almost filled the room.

Jude I know. Thank you for doing that. Me and Acton, we drifted apart after our mother's death. Or before then too, maybe.

Frayne Acton never said you lost contact.

Hoke But then again, Acton didn't say much. When he was a kid you couldn't shut him up.

Jude How was his health?

Frayne (*shrugs*) Like all of us he drank some, went to the gym some. Normal, some, I guess.

Jude Did he have a girlfriend?

Hoke I don't know. Frayne?

Frayne He had this one redhead for a while. A few years back.

Hoke Right: Lou. I knew that. Pretty. Too skinny though.

Frayne He said Lou used to bite him.

Hoke Ouch.

Frayne He said he liked it at first. But then he started pushing her to bite harder till she took off a piece of his ear.

Hoke Jesus.

Frayne Just a little piece but she left after that.

Hoke Your brother was a quiet man but he worked hard. Right in our building, for years.

Jude What did he do for you?

Hoke He was one of our. Engineers. At my offices, and for the hospitals.

Jude An engineer? Well, good for him. That's quite impressive.

Frayne Maintenance engineer.

Jude Oh?

Frayne AC. Windows. Heat.

Hoke He was an All Around.

Jude (*nods*) A handyman.

Hoke I kept Acton in a job just like I promised back then. Back here. Right here.

Jude You promised him a job like your job. What exactly is your job?

Hoke Family business.

Frayne Big family business.

Hoke Health First. COO.

Jude whistles in admiration. Hoke shrugs.

Jude (*to Frayne*) He's your boss too?

28

Hoke It's Hoke, not 'he'.

Frayne Used to be.

Hoke Ingrate.

Frayne Now I'm an engineer of domestic hydrology.

Hoke Plumber.

Frayne Plumber's assistant.

Jude What's that?

Frayne Eight thousand a year less.

Hoke He grapples with shit day in and day out.

Frayne (*to Jude*) And what do you do?

Jude I grapple with shit too. Mostly appliances.

Frayne Electrician? Not bad.

Jude Not certified. So I work at the small stuff, dirty stuff, for folks who pay in cash or kind. Crooks too, 'cause they give better tips.

Hoke (*laughs*) Still the same Jude. I'm glad. (*Beat.*) Look. We lost contact with Acton too, in the last few years. But he was always like a brother.

Frayne I saw him a couple of weeks before he died.

Hoke What? No you didn't /

Frayne (*cuts him off*) Yeah. Pale, his face was. Transparent almost. Like I could reach out and put my hand through /

Hoke You didn't tell me you saw him again.

Frayne I just saw him for a few. We bumped into each other on Third and Chestnut.

Hoke Oh. (*Beat.*) I'll take you up on that sandwich, Jude. If you got wholewheat bread it'd be perfect.

Jude Just white.

Hoke Almost perfect. With a pickle?

Jude Got that. Why don't you all come on up and we'll picnic on the porch.

Frayne (*to Jude*) He still looked like you. As a matter of fact Acton looked more like you than he did as a kid, more like you than you are now /

Hoke Frayne. That's enough.

Frayne It'd been a few years since I last saw him and I meant to say, 'How are you, Acton?' but I got my words wrong and I said, 'How are you, Jude?' He said, 'I'm just fine.' He didn't miss a beat.

SCENE THREE

Diggs' basement. 1977. September.
    Hoke, Acton and Frayne, late at night. The boys are under sheets, in various states of sleep.

Hoke Frayne! Hey. Acton.

Acton Shhh.

Hoke We got to talk. Now!

Acton You'll wake my mom.

   Hoke switches on a small flashlight under his sheet.

Hoke Get up, Frayne.

Frayne Fuck off, I'm asleep.

Hoke I've got it.

Acton Shhh. Got what, Hoke?

Frayne A hard-on? Put those damn magazines away or I'll burn 'em.

Hoke I'm going to fail my SATs next week.

Frayne Jesus Christ, not again.

Hoke I am.

Acton switches on his flashlight.

Acton No you're not – cause I've been tutoring you for weeks. Quit worrying.

Hoke uncovers himself.

Hoke I'm gonna fail my SATs.

Frayne switches on his light.

Frayne How many times we got to go over this?

Hoke On purpose. I'm going to fail them on purpose.

Frayne and Acton now uncover themselves.

Frayne What do you mean?

Acton On purpose?

Hoke Exactly that. Now listen: Frayne, you fucked me over big time when you told Mr Carolson in Civics last week that that was my joint under your chair.

Frayne But it was! It fell out of your bag!

Hoke So what? You didn't have my back.

Frayne How many times do I have to say I'm sorry, huh?

Hoke The point is I forgave you for not lying for me.

Frayne The point is your dad only had to open his mouth to the principal and all was forgiven.

Hoke Still, you let me down.

Frayne Yeah? What about the time you drove over our mailbox. On purpose. Did you get me a new one? No. My dad grounded me for two weeks. You let *me* down.

Hoke Yes. I did. This is what I'm talking about. At some point or other, we all let each other down. It can't be helped.

Acton I haven't let either of you down.

Hoke But you will.

Acton I won't.

Hoke You might. And that might is an ever present threat.
  So I been thinking that what we lack is solid evidence that our friendship, our alliance, is unbreakable no matter what shit comes our way. So I'm going to fail my tests.

Acton That's stupid.

Frayne That's fucked up.

Hoke That's sac-ri-fice. I'm going to show both of you how much you matter, how much 'we' matter, by giving up the best thing I got: my ticket to the Ivy League.

Acton But we don't want you to give that up. Do we, Frayne?

Frayne Course not.

Hoke By this. Act. This offering, I'll give up something important to the greater good, the greater love. I'll give proof that for me our bond is. Authentic. To the bone. Look, we eat together, we party together, we jerk off together /

Acton I don't do that.

Hoke You try, same thing. We share every little secret we got together, but where's the glue to hold fast when there's a bump? I need to give up my SATs. It'll hurt, but I want to hurt. For you. And you.

Frayne He's stoned.

Acton Maybe he's sick?

Hoke I feel great just thinking about it. For every answer I know on the exams, I'm going to mark the opposite. I'm going to . . . impeach my own damn self!

Hoke steps up and begins to preach, the sheet still draped around his shoulders.

Whatever happens out there, whatever lies ahead in this uncertain terrain of . . . wolverines, this bond will be our life jacket, our own homegrown Watergate and law unto ourselves. We will shore up against insecurity and doubt. No Tricky Dicks for us, no Cong, no Laos will bring us low /

Frayne Shhhh!

Acton Jude's gonna hear us.

Hoke No Rusty Calley will knock at our door to rub our faces in shit and shame! Let the fuckin' misery index rise so high it hits the clouds, it. Will. Not. Come. Nigh. Thee!

Silence. Hoke is pleased with himself.

'Thee' meaning 'us' as 'you' means 'me'.

Acton Your mom and dad are gonna kill you.

Hoke Yeah. They kind of have their hearts set on Yale. I feel. You know, right now I feel.

Frayne What?

Hoke I feel . . . 'Nights'!

Hoke begins to dance/sway with the sheet, whisper-singing 'Nights in White Satin' by the Moody Blues. They all join in, and sing: 'How I love you!'

Shit.

Frayne What?

Hoke Now I've got a boner.

Frayne Christ.

Hoke This big decision's stirred me up. Wow. Kind of hurts.

Acton Can we go back to sleep now? We've got school tomorrow.

Hoke You're next, Frayne.

Frayne Huh?

Hoke How are you gonna prove your bond? I'm gonna give up my SATs. Top that. T-M-L. Top My Love.

Frayne I'm not failing my SATs. My folks been saving for college since I was born.

Hoke Can't do the same thing as me anyway. But we have to make it hurt. We have to make our insides pop. And then we'll float, rise up, like Jonathan Livingston Fucking Seagull!

Frayne Sure. Now let's get some sleep, damn it.

The boys get back under their sheets. Their flashlights go out one by one.

Acton I could sacrifice my guitar. I could let you smash it up.

Frayne You love that guitar.

Acton Yeah. I touch it every day, more than I touch anything.

Hoke Wait your turn, little bro. Frayne goes next.

Silence a moment.

Acton I can't give up Skimpy. Skimpy's sick anyway. She's got tumors 'cause she's old.

Frayne That's kind of gross, Acton, to have feelings for a rat.

Acton The tumors are growing so fast in her belly that they're lifting her up from underneath and now it's like she's sitting on a throne of tumors.

34

Hoke The vet should put that thing down.

Acton But she's not in pain. Jude says Skimpy thinks the tumors are just a normal part of her.

Frayne Sleep, okay!

Acton Skimpy doesn't know she's sick so she's not afraid; doesn't even know she's dying.

SCENE FOUR

Frayne and Hoke on the Diggs' empty porch. 1991. Same night. Some minutes later.

Hoke Carol's making ribs on Sunday.

Frayne Her garlic ribs? Shit. I'll be there early.

Hoke Eight p.m., if that's not too late. Kids have soccer.

Hoke suddenly grabs Frayne by the throat. Frayne hardly reacts. They are both wary that they not be overheard.

What do you mean by 'transparent'? Huh? Huh?

Frayne It's just a word that came to me. Shit.

Hoke shoves Frayne away.

Hoke Well use another word. *Transparent.* Jesus. What are you trying to do, create an atmosphere?

Frayne We already got an atmosphere.

Hoke Hey. I object to your mysterious and leading tone, so quit it. There's not a thing that's not clear, okay?

Frayne Therefore my word: transparent.

Hoke I'm warning you.

Frayne Hoke. It's only normal she's got questions.

Hoke I don't have questions. There's the Ohio river. There's the bridge. There's Acton who fucked us both over by hurling himself from that same bridge during rush hour. As public as he could be. Jesus. There were kids who saw it. And his last howdie-do to this world? His slippers left behind on the bridge railing. Not shoes, no. Slippers. Acton walked to the bridge in his slippers. Why not put on some goddamn shoes?

Frayne When was the last time you talked to him?

Hoke A few months back.

Frayne What did he say?

Hoke 'How you doin', Hoke?' I said 'Great, how you doin', Acton?' That's been our level for years now and you know it. (*Beat.*) She's still a beauty, our Jude is. Huh. What did you used to call her?

Frayne *Bitch*. 'Cause she was always yelling at us to keep it down. *Fuckin' bitch* when she'd kick us out of the basement just for the hell of it.

Hoke You had other words for her then.

Frayne Don't you ever just want to /

Hoke No, I don't.

Frayne But we could be free of /

Hoke I am free, Frayne. I feel very free.

Frayne You're lying. Maybe we could just talk about a piece of it.

Hoke It.

Frayne You brought up the party.

Hoke That's just reminiscing. If done with care, reminiscing is harmless.

Frayne You don't dream about it?

Hoke doesn't respond.

I wake up sweatin' 'cause something always goes wrong.

Hoke Nothing went wrong.

Frayne And it's dark and it's like there's this huge zipper running straight down my back and all of a sudden someone, something, grabs hold of it and jerks the zipper down and my back just opens up and spills out all over.

Hoke Wow, that's disgusting. (*Beat.*) But I bet you still wake up hard.

Frayne No. I don't.

Hoke Now you're lying. Admit that you still fantasize /

Frayne Shut up.

Hoke Still jerk off /

Frayne If you don't shut your mouth.

Hoke Okay, okay.

They are silent some moments.

I miss /

Frayne Acton. Yeah. Me too.

Hoke When it was just the three of us, here. Even Jude was fun sometimes back then. Man, I loved being a kid.

Frayne Didn't last long enough.

Hoke Tick, tick, tick the years go by and all too soon I'm head of one of the most powerful health insurance companies in the country and I feel . . .

Frayne Rich? Very rich?

Hoke Bored.

Frayne Fuck you. Go bore yourself to death. Jesus.

Hoke Look, Frayne. I am trying to share an emotional moment with you because you're still my best friend and I love you. So what's up?

Frayne The beginning of it was wrong.

Hoke Things like that happen all the time. People move on.

Frayne Acton didn't move on.

Hoke Acton was an asthmatic, scrawny, bullied brat when we scraped him up off the locker-room tiles way back when. We gave him the best months of his life. He said so himself, repeatedly, remember? And when we grew up, we kept our promises.

Frayne We kept our secrets.

Hoke Same thing. Look, the kid lost his dad when he was twelve. No one survives that intact. When Acton turned eighteen, my dad put him on the best fuckin' medication money can buy and didn't charge him a cent and a few years ago I put him on the new stuff. And these new meds, fuckin' hell, they're like guided missiles. Smart bombs. They pinpoint the wound with phenomenal accuracy and then obliterate it, without touching the rest.

Frayne The autopsy showed Acton had no drugs of any kind in his body.

Hoke Exactly. When we bumped into each other that last time, in my building, he was putting in a new window, he said to me, Acton said, 'Those pills kill the pain.' I said, 'Then they're working.' He said, 'I'm living but I'm kinda dead too.' I said, 'It's okay to be a little bit dead as long as you're alive.' We laughed at that. He said, 'But the pills are punching out my lights.' I said, 'Buy some candles.'

Frayne Okay. Stop it.

Hoke Acton said, 'But I've got to feel, and I can't like this.'

Frayne I don't want to hear /

Hoke I said, 'You've felt enough, Acton. Let it go.' I put my arm on his arm. I gave him my best counsel. He looked into my eyes and I looked into his and I felt like we were having a moment, the first real moment since way back when, until I became aware of something on my shoe. (*Beat.*) He was pissing on my shoe.

Frayne What the hell?! Is that why you fired him?

Hoke No one pisses on my shoe, in my own building, in public. You want to piss on my shoe, do it in private. Privatize that kind of fucking behavior. We're in the midst of a tech explosion. Kaboom! Who can't be happy? It's raining opportunity and all you have to do is hold out your arms and let 'em fill up. Acton resisted opportunity at every turn.

Jude enters, carrying in her hands sandwiches and beers for Hoke and Frayne, but until she speaks they don't see her. She's changed into more comfortable clothes.

He missed the call, missed the bell. Cong, Cong, Cong. Damn, I long for that word: Cong. Vietcong. You never hear that word anymore. We grew up on a war and we knew it but it hardly touched us.

Frayne Just finished another one and it's hardly touched us.

Jude (*appears to them*) Wholewheat after all. Mayo and cheese. Provolone and pickles. The pickles gone soft but they're still good.

Hoke Delicious.

Jude What hardly touched us?

Frayne The war.

Hoke Hmmm. This is nice.

Jude (*casually*) Which one?

Hoke (*eating*) Frayne and I, we were just reminiscing about our sweet birds of youth. And our birds were, let's admit it, sorely intimidated by yours, Jude.

Jude Well you were shy. It was easy to intimidate you.

Hoke I wasn't shy.

Jude With girls. With me.

Hoke You made up words to impress us.

Jude I learned words –

Frayne – to scare us.

Jude And it worked.

Hoke Smart as an encyclopedia.

Jude I read the whole row of blue-backed *Encyclopedia Britannica*, all the way up to S.

Frayne What happened at S?

Jude The books came in every few months. Mail order. My parents gave me a subscription for my eleventh birthday. I was going to be an anthropologist.

Frayne I thought it was geologist?

Jude Maybe it was. But the books weren't cheap. So when my dad died, Mom cancelled the order. Then she cancelled Acton's guitar lessons, the once-a-year, four-day cabin rental at Taylorsville Lake, the fresh fruit, dentists, the /

Hoke Okay, Jude. We get it.

Jude We had to count our pennies. Most everyone did back then.
(*To Hoke.*) But not Hoke.

Hoke Guilty as charged and I don't feel a lick of shame about it either.

Frayne My folks counted their dimes but we kept the fresh fruit.

Hoke Hey. You listen to me, my family –

Frayne – worked their asses off for generations, yeah, we know.

Hoke I was going to say most of them inherited their wealth. The rest knew how to pull a good string when they saw one. (*Beat.*) If I was shy with you, Judith, well. You were . . . formidable. Wasn't she, Frayne?

Frayne That she was.

Hoke You and your girl friends used to come down to the basement –

Frayne – slap on Clapton and dance, dance –

Hoke – and we'd just sit and watch all that e-lec-tricity spark, and we were mesmerized –

Frayne – sweatin' static till we were lit up too.

Hoke And darlin', you were as tart and single-minded –

Frayne –as a bottle rocket on the Fourth of July.

Jude Yeah. I was, wasn't I?

SCENE FIVE

Jude and Acton alone in the Diggs' basement. 1977. November. Acton is trying to teach Jude some chords.

Acton You're fighting the strings.

Jude Little bastards are fighting me!

Acton You're pressing too hard. Try G again.

Jude gives Acton back his guitar.

Jude Electric's out in five days from Sunday if I don't pay it. Last paycheck went to your new shoes and –

Acton – and they love my feet.

Jude Mom's barely making the rent . . . But as she says, better to have a home without lights than –

Jude *and* **Acton** Lights without a home.

Jude Listen, Acton, if I /

Acton (*cuts her off*) No way, Jude.

Jude Then I could get a full-time job.

Acton If you quit, I quit.

Jude Law says you can't quit till you're fifteen. I can quit school now.

Acton If you quit school you'll turn out just like Mom.

Jude Mom's workin' two jobs, Acton.

Acton Yeah, and she's the saddest person I know besides my sister.

Jude (*laughs*) I'm not sad.

Acton uses his inhaler.

Acton Maybe we should do like Mom says and move to Florida and live with Granny.

Jude No. We're staying here. This is our home. Look, Acton, the world's a hard place and people /

Acton Yeah, and people slip off it.

Acton plays some discordant notes on his guitar.

Jude Dad didn't slip. His harness broke. Quit that! Dad had phenomenal balance.

Jude snatches away Acton's guitar.

When the ice was so hard on the pond and you could drive a tractor on it, me and you and Mom, we'd be sloppin' and sloshin' around on our skates like water in a pan, Dad would be gliding his way round the edge, his skates like knives –

Acton – criss-cross, criss-cross.

Jude Yeah. And when we fell he'd sweep on by and scoop us up in his arms like sacks of 'taters.

Acton What do you think Dad was thinking about when he was falling?

Jude I can't now, Acton. I got to get ready for work.

Acton Come on. Just a few. (*Beat.*) You like to do it. Dad would've liked us to do it.

Jude Okay. But quick.

They play their 'game', making it up as they go along, but they keep the pace flowing.

Jude When Dad was falling, he was thinkin': *Damn, double damn. I didn't get to eat my lunch. Velveeta –*

Acton – *on rye and a pickle. Shit. There goes my best arm!*

Jude *And my favorite drink: Orange Crush! Orange –*

Acton – *Crush! I'm flyin' like a bird, no, like a brick from the fourteenth floor.* Dad's thinking:

Jude *I shoulda put fresh socks on this morning.*

Acton *I'm upside down, spinnin' like a top. Is someone gonna –*

Jude – *catch me? Catch me or bye, bye, birdie.*
(*Sings.*) *'I saw you today at the reception.'*

Acton *My tank's on empty, will they find the keys?*

Jude *'I'm gonna meet my connection.'*
  (Speaks.) Concrete!

Acton *Bye, bye, Jude. Bye, bye,*

Jude *Acton. Bye, bye, sweet soon-to-be-widowed wife.*

Acton *The sidewalk's rushing up way too fast –*

Jude *This bird is gonna bust.*

Acton *I'm dead!*

Jude *Dead!*

Jude *and* **Acton** *Dead!*

Jude Want me to get you some ice tea 'fore I go? I made it extra sweet.

  Acton doesn't respond.

I can ride this pony, Acton. No matter how hard the bitch bucks, I'm not coming off.

Acton But what if I do?

Jude I won't let you.

Acton Dad fell off.

Jude Yeah, but now things are different. Now it's me keeping this family whole. *(Beat.)* Trust me. I'll make it work for the three of us, I promise.

Acton Okay.

Jude I promise.

  Silence a moment.

Acton Oh. Frayne wants me to ask you, without you knowing he wants me to ask you, if you like him.

  Now Jude changes, putting on her work clothes over her regular ones.

Jude Frayne? He's mean, shallow, an only half-smart bastard. Tell him when you asked me I laughed so hard I farted.

Acton I'll tell him there's hope.

Jude There's no hope.

Acton I don't mind if you like him but Hoke doesn't know that Frayne asked me to ask you so don't tell him.

Jude He's got okay feet.

Acton Can I tell him you said so?

Jude No. And big hands that don't shake.

Acton He's got a serious crush on you. Then so does the whole school.

Jude Yeah, but they don't know me. Tell Frayne I'll give him a kiss, an almost-real one on the mouth, on my birthday, if he brings a case of Pabst and comes barefoot.

Acton In November? At a field party?

Jude He'll have to risk the frostbite.

Acton Hoke says he's gonna get me a job soon as I'm out of school.

Jude You'll get a scholarship if you keep up your grades. What kind of job?

Acton The kind that'll let me buy Mom a real house.

Jude This is a real house.

Acton Hoke's basement's got a pool table, a bar, a gym with weights and a stationary bike. You can run laps round his basement.

Jude Losers own stationary bikes.

Acton The lights don't go out at Hoke's. He says they never even think about lights.

Jude I gotta go. Make sure you heat up Mom's dinner 'fore she gets home from work. It's on the stove.

Acton But what if Mom gets hit by a car or you're walking in a storm and a branch falls and breaks your neck.

Jude Acton. I'm not going to die. Neither is Mom.

Acton Swear to me.

Jude Borborygmus.

Acton Borborygmus. Ever and ever.

Jude Amen.

Acton What's it mean?

Jude An intestinal rumbling caused by gas.

Acton Cool. (*Beat.*) You don't really want me to tell Frayne you farted when you laughed?

Jude Sure.

Acton Then I'll tell him your farts are the worst.

Jude My farts are royal, stand-alone winners, and when a tree falls in the forest, you know why. Tell him. Then we'll see how much he luuuves me.

Acton You're gross.

Jude They've got a lot in common, love and farts. They both come forth from the darkest holes and smell like shit. But watch out. They pack an almighty punch when you least expect it. So don't mess with 'em. And don't –

Jude *and* **Acton** – mess with me.

Jude and Acton give each other a high five.

SCENE SIX

Jude, Hoke and Frayne on the Diggs' porch. 1991. Dusk. Same evening. Young Jude passes them on her way to work, buttoning up her work shirt.

Jude (*calmly*) I'm just irritated, not angry. Such an obvious symmetry with my father's death. Though Acton dove rather than fell. Now if my brother had thrown himself onto the Belle's ruddy blades as it chugged up the river, that would have given us food for thought /

Hoke Quit. You don't have to play tough-ass with us. We're all hurt by his death.

Jude Hurt. Such a small word. It's more like a . . . a cold humming inside, sharp enough to cut glass.

Hoke Well, I'm just plain old sad.

Jude Of course you are.

Frayne Listen. I want to. I want to talk about Jude's seventeenth.

Hoke We already talked about that party.

Frayne I want to talk about it again.

Hoke (*warning*) Frayne.

Jude Sure. Go ahead.

Frayne (*to Jude*) Okay. Right. Well, that night you were like a rag doll dipped in Jim Beam.

Jude Sure. I'd had too much to drink.

Hoke All a blur to me.

Frayne We found you passed out in the basement. Right, Hoke?

Hoke gives Frayne a warning look but Frayne ignores him.

47

Your girlfriends tucked you up safe, then they went back to the party. We dared each other. You were alone.

Jude Dared each other . . .?

Hoke Yes. We dared each other to feel you. Up.

Jude (*curious*) When I was unconscious?

Hoke *and* **Frayne** Yeah.

Jude What. Exactly happened?

Frayne You tell her, Hoke.

Hoke Jesus . . . Okay: we felt your tits.

Frayne On top of your shirt, not under.

They are silent a moment. Jude remains calm.

Jude Oh. Okay. What else?

Hoke I went first. For the tits part. Then Frayne, he.

Frayne Then I did that. Too. Then we felt between your legs.

Hoke (*to Frayne*) You went first on that one.

Frayne Yeah, I did.

Hoke Just a couple rubs *on top* of your jeans, between your.

Frayne Not under them. Not under the jeans: no skin.

Hoke Then we left. We felt bad, feeling you up, we felt –

Hoke quits. They wait some moments, in an uncomfortable silence.

Jude And where was Acton?

Frayne Hoke gave Acton the keys to his Firebird.

Hoke I sent him to get us a twelve-pack. If Acton had known.

Hoke shakes his head.

Frayne He'd've killed us.

Hoke We'd like to say we're sorry, Jude.

Frayne Yeah. We're sorry.

Hoke It was a stupid, drunken –

Frayne Prank. Fucked up and wrong.

Hoke Dead wrong and we knew it then. We know it now.

Jude takes this in. They wait.

Jude I suppose worse things than a quick feel can happen when you're passed out among friends, right?

Hoke Jude, you were a queen. We were just kids who saw an opportunity and we took it. We knew we'd never get another chance to touch you. Opportunistic bastards.

Jude Yes. You were. Rascals. Little devils. (*Beat.*) Do you feel better now?

Hoke I think I do. Frayne?

Frayne doesn't reply.

Listen. If there's a way to make it up to you /

Jude I'll need to stay here for a while to clear out the house, so some kind of work to hold me over would be helpful. Or maybe I'll keep the house and send for Linda. We could live here if I had a decent job.

Hoke Define decent.

Jude Thirty thousand a year start pay?

Hoke Can you type, file and make a pot of killer coffee?

Jude Yes-siree.

Frayne Pull a string, Hoke.

49

Hoke I'll see what I can do. But it won't be because of what we did.

Jude Oh? Why then?

Hoke Because this is the first time you've ever asked me for a favor.

Frayne Me, I don't have much. Can't give you a job.

Jude We'll think of something else then, won't we?

Hoke Now Jude. Give us a little break here. We didn't have to tell you. And it's not like you were totally innocent, then.

Jude Ah.

Hoke You told us so yourself.

Frayne All things considered, what we did that night was –

Hoke Comparatively speaking . . . Transparent?

Jude Superficial?

Jude is silent a moment.

Oh hell. What the fuck. Yeah, okay. Look, I'm gonna drive up to Neffs and get some more beer. You'll stay a little longer won't you, and join me?

Hoke Sure, but no booze. Got a flight to Atlanta tomorrow early. Six thirty-five a.m.

Jude (*to Frayne*) How 'bout you?

Frayne I can stay.

Jude (*nods*) I'll be back in fifteen. Help yourselves to anything in the kitchen if you're still hungry. (*Beat.*) Oh, I'll need a car.

Hoke and Frayne don't respond.

Not just tonight, but for whatever time I'm here.

Frayne I don't have a car.

Hoke He's got a truck.
  (*To Frayne.*) Piece of shit but four new tires you said, right?

Jude Ford?

Hoke Never drives anything else.

Jude I'll take it.

Jude holds out her hand for the truck keys. Frayne slowly gets them out of his jeans pocket, keeping his eyes on Jude. Frayne drops the keys in her hand just as the three youths – Acton, Jude and Frayne – come barreling past. Their older selves do not see them.

SCENE SEVEN

Jude and Acton surround Frayne in the Diggs' basement.
  Later in November. 1977.
Frayne has a makeshift bandage around his hand. There's some dried blood on it.

Jude What the hell happened?

Frayne attempts to hide his hand.

Acton Let me see.

Frayne Not yet.

Jude Hold still.

Frayne Where's Hoke?!

Jude grabs Frayne's hand and slowly unwraps it. Frayne tries not to wince.

Acton Hoke's on his way. Wow. That's impressive.

Jude You'll need a doctor to look at that.

Jude pokes at the wound. Frayne lets out a howl, but it's more of triumph than pain.

Acton Hurts bad, huh?

Frayne Kinda. Yeah.

Jude How'd you do it?

Acton You're gonna have a scar.

Jude raises Frayne's hand and gently kisses his palm. He winces slightly.

(*To Jude.*) Euw. There's blood on your lip.

Frayne Do that again?

Hoke bursts in.

Hoke What'd you do, Frayne?

Frayne I Topped That. T- Y- L. I Topped Your Love. (*To Acton.*) And yours.

Hoke Cough it up then.

Jude What? It's this stupid game again?

Acton It's not a game, Jude.

Jude Damn you. Shit.

Jude deliberately wipes her lips, her eyes on Frayne.

Hoke It's a *relinquishing*. A giving.

Frayne A goddamn sac-ri-fice. Look at the holes in my hand!

Acton (*counting*) There's five of 'em.

Hoke examines Frayne's hand.

Hoke Jesus. Bite marks?

Frayne These, my friends, are the marks of my commitment. (*Beat.*) So, last night, late, I go down to the kitchen.

Jude Losers.

Frayne My mom and dad are /

Jude You're fuckin' losers.

Frayne (*suddenly*) Back off, bitch. No one wants you here anyway.

Jude tries to attack Frayne. Frayne doesn't respond, just smiles at her while Hoke and Acton hold Jude back.

Hoke *and* **Acton** Hey! Stop it. Get off him. Calm down, Jude.

Jude moves away from them, but still listens. Frayne continues.

Frayne So, my mom and dad are asleep. My brother Terry's in his wheelchair in the living room. Terry usually sleeps in his chair but he's awake and he's watching a re-run of *Lost in Space* and I'm figuring I need a witness, but one who can't talk, so I turn Terry's chair to face the kitchen and I get me one of those real big forks.

Acton Oh no.

Hoke Shhh.

Frayne Oh yeah, the kind you use only once a year to serve up hot turkey and I lay my hand, palm up, on the cutting board and I say, 'Terry. I know what it feels like, brother,' and I give him a wink. Then I bring that fork down on my hand like a fuckin' B-52 –

Frayne *and* **Hoke** – gravity bomb.

Acton Whoa.

Hoke That took some guts.

Jude I'm going to report you.

Hoke But self-mutilation doesn't count, Frayne.

Jude But to who? The principal?

Frayne Acton. Get rid of your sis for us, please?

Jude The cops? I'll tell the cops.

Acton Don't be stupid, Jude.

Jude Or maybe your parents?

Acton You can't.

Frayne No one cares what we do.

Hoke Jude. If you tell anyone, so help me /

Frayne Shut the hell up! All of you. That's just Part One. 'Cause well, Terry, he starts crying in that roller coaster way, seeing what I did and how I'm bleeding and I start cryin' too 'cause it hurts like hell and Mom and Dad come running down the stairs in their matchin' PJs. 'What happened? Oh my Gawd, what happened?' And that's when I say it, 'Creek bit me.' At first they can't believe it 'cause our dog Creek never bit a flea but then I elaborate on how I was just innocently scratchin' him behind his ears and suddenly he reaches round and chomps my hand. Poor Creek. All the while I'm lying about him, his tail's waggin' 'cause he's hearin' his name. Well, you know what comes next. Mom says to Dad, 'I don't want that dog in my house. Take him to the pound first thing in the morning.' I say: (*Mocks himself.*) 'No, no, Creek's my dog! I won't let you take him,' but I know Mom won't budge.

Acton Creek's a really cool dog.

Frayne Yep. Had him since I was eight. Sleeps on my bed with his nose in my ear. Still, while I'm bawlin' and my hand's bleedin', I'm thinking Creek's a beautiful dog, big, so black he's blue, half-collie, no way someone won't adopt him quick, as it's only his first offense.

Jude But Creek didn't bite you, asshole. You lied.

Hoke Course he lied. Just like I lied when I failed my SATs and told my parents I had no idea what went wrong 'cause I'd studied my ass off.

Acton *I* studied my ass off for you, / Hoke.

Frayne Jesus, let me finish! Next morning I figure I'll take Creek to the pound myself so I can scratch his head and tell him I'm sorry on the way over and explain to him why it had to be done. So I'm callin' Creek in the yard 'cause he's usually out there in the morning takin' a piss and Dad's already up slurpin' on his coffee and he says, 'I buried Creek last night.' I say, 'What do you mean?' You know, you say stupid shit like that to hold it off and Dad says, 'No dog bites my boy.' I go out in the grass and it's wet and I'm barefoot. There's a fresh Creek-sized grave dug at the back of the yard. Shovel lying next to it.

They are all silent some moments, taking this in.

(*Quietly.*) Top that.

Hoke Damn right, top that. Shit. Shit!

Acton (*mesmerized*) Was there blood on the shovel?

Jude Acton, go to your room.

Hoke Wow. Top that!

Acton Jude.

Hoke Top My Love!

Jude Go to your room now.

Acton No.

Jude No?

Frayne (*quietly*) Let him stay, Jude.

Jude Frayne. You're sick. Sick! Both of you bastards /

Acton (*cuts her off*) Don't talk to my friends like that. Don't you dare! Just like Frayne says. I used to tell him not to say it but it's true: You're not just a bitch. You're a. A. Cunt.

Frayne Hey. I never said /

Jude Acton . . .?

Acton explodes.

Acton Did you even hear what Frayne did? Did you hear? Open your fuckin' ears /

Jude Don't you talk to me like /

Acton (*cuts her off*) Frayne did it for *us*! For Hoke. To prove. For me. To. Have you ever done something like that? Have you? No. No! You never have 'cause it's. He loved that dog! It's. It's.

Acton suddenly quiets. Jude just stares at Acton, then walks out. The boys are silent a moment.

Acton (*quietly*) It's perfect.

Hoke It is. So let's celebrate.

Acton Yeah. Let's celebrate.

Acton takes a joint out of its hiding place.

I've been saving this for something special.

Hoke grabs the joint from Acton.

Hoke Where'd you get this?

Acton My dad had a bad back from work. Took me months to find it, hid in a minnow bucket. It's kinda dry now but I bet it's good.

Frayne Well let's light her up. I haven't had a smoke in weeks.

They smoke the joint together as they talk.

Hoke Not bad. Not bad at all.

Frayne Your daddy had good taste in weed. So. It's your turn. Whatcha gonna give us, little brother?

Hoke Yeah. Whatcha gonna give us?

SCENE EIGHT

A few days later. Night. 1977. Footsteps. Jude turns on the porch light and finds Acton crouched down, huddled over an old suitcase.

Jude Acton. What the hell. What are you –

Jude puts her hand on his shoulder but he shakes it off.

You're shivering. Come back inside.

Now Jude sees the suitcase.

What's the suitcase for? (*Beat.*) Acton!

Acton I'm leaving.

Jude (*stays calm*) Okay. Why?

Acton I'm gonna live with Granny in Florida. She says the heat helps with the arthritis but she misses us bad.

Jude What happened?

Acton She wrote on a card she'll buy me a fishing rod. A real one with a spin cast.

Jude It's those bastards again, isn't it?

Acton I got to start walking.

Jude You're gonna walk to Florida?

Acton No, to the bus stop. Mom gave me the bus money to go.

Jude She did not.

Acton I told her I'd hitchhike if she didn't.

Jude Give me that!

Jude tries to take the suitcase from him but he holds on to it.

Acton Jude. I'm leaving.

Jude No.

Acton Hoke says David Cassidy left home when he was younger than me.

He sings from 'Rock Me Baby'.

Jude Cassidy didn't even write that song.

Acton You mean he lied?

Jude You can't leave. Mom needs you here. I do too. Look, if you come in I'll make you hot chocolate. And play the falling game.

Acton considers this some moments.

Acton Let's play it here. Now.

Jude takes a deep breath.

Jude You start.

Acton When Dad was falling he was thinking: *I can taste the hard-boiled egg I had for breakfast.*

Jude *The sky is . . . colossal and the clouds are gonna pop.*

Acton *Pop. How come they never called me Pop?*

Jude *Just Dad and Daddy. Can anyone see me?*

Acton *I see people lookin' up.*

Jude *Hey! Don't just stand there, open your arms, catch me!*

Acton doesn't join in the finale.

Catch me!!

After a moment:

Acton 'You have to kill Skimpy.' That's what they said to me.

Jude What? What do you mean, kill Skimpy?

Acton Frayne offered to break her neck quick but Skimpy's neck's so small and his hands are so big.

Jude I'm going to beat the shit out of both of them.

Acton Hoke said we could put her in a glass jar with a couple of peanuts and pitch her into the river and that at least she'd have a wild boat ride before the jar broke but Skimpy's afraid of water.

Jude We've got to tell Mom about this, Acton. It has to stop.

Acton But in the end they both agreed Skimpy was just vermin. I hate that word. So said: my guitar.

Jude No! You listen to me: you're talented, Acton. You need that guitar. I am not lettin' them take your guitar.

Acton Not my guitar. You.

Jude What?

Acton I have to give them you.

Jude Me?

Acton Hoke lost Yale. Frayne lost Creek.

Jude Me?

Acton Hoke says it has to be a step up from a dog and that's not a rat or guitar.

Jude Give them *me*? What the hell /

59

Acton I told them 'no'. I said, 'No way.'

Jude How do they think you can. Give me?

Acton You're not supposed to know.
(*Suddenly afraid.*) Please don't tell them, Jude. They'll /

Jude Those sons of bitches . . .

Acton Hoke says if I don't do it they'll throw me to the wolves.

Jude There are no wolves around / here.

Acton Duh. He means throw me to the bullies. And there are more of them now and they hate me twice as bad 'cause I got protection. So I have to go to Florida and you have to stay behind and take care of Mom and Skimpy.

Jude How was this supposed to happen without you telling me?

Acton Hoke has a pill that can knock a cow off its feet in under three minutes.

Jude A pill?

Acton He stole it from his dad's office. It dissolves in water and has almost no taste and no headache in the morning either. I'm supposed to put a pill in your beer at the party next week.

Jude At my birthday party?

Acton Yeah . . .

Jude Without my knowing it?

Acton Yeah. And then when you're passed out. They would.

Jude Both of them?

Acton Yeah.

Jude Here? In our basement?

Acton Yeah.

Jude Huh.

Acton Hoke said you'd never know and Frayne said you wouldn't feel a thing and they'd be really careful so when you woke up you wouldn't notice they'd.

Jude They'd . . .?

Acton That's why I'm leaving. 'Cause I said *No*. And 'cause I said no, I'll be pulped every day for the rest of my life /

Jude You really talked about this with them.

Acton Please don't be mad at me, Jude. Please /

Jude Be quiet.

Acton I said to Hoke and Frayne, 'No way.' I said it over and over, 'No way, no way, no way.' More than that even. (*Beat.*) Jude?

Jude (*trying to think*) Shut up.

> *Acton gets up, ready to go.*

Acton I gotta go now, Jude. If I catch the night bus, Granny says I can sleep through the drive and be walkin' on the beach by morning.

> *After some moments, Jude comes to a decision.*

Jude I'll do it.

Acton Huh?

Jude I'll do it.

Acton What do you mean?

Jude You got the pill?

Acton Hoke's got it. But you can't /

Jude (*cuts him off*) Just listen. Here's the plan: tomorrow morning you call Hoke and Frayne, tell them you're in. Get the cow pill from Hoke and tell him that at the end of the party, you'll bring me down to the basement, telling me you got a special birthday present but you want to give it to me in private. I'll act like I'm drunk 'cause it's my party and if I'm not drunk they'll suspect something. You put the pill in my beer and when I'm out cold, you let Hoke and Frayne in. They get twenty minutes with me. No, fifteen. That's it. And you make sure you time it too. Don't budge on the time. Then they're done and you kick 'em out. (*Beat.*) But first, they got to agree to protect you till school's over, and second, they never set foot in this house again. Ever.

Acton What if they won't agree?

Jude They will. They know they'll never get it any other way.

Acton If they find out we planned it together, it won't count.

Jude They won't find out. And none of us is going to Florida. The three of us, you, me and Mom, our home is right here. No one is going to split us up.

Acton You'd really do this for me?

After a moment:

Jude Yeah. If you promise to stay.

Acton thinks about this. Jude waits.

Acton I promise. But. But I won't let you do it, Jude. No, no way!

For a moment, Jude feels a flood of relief. She looks at her brother and smiles.

I mean I will let you do it, but I don't want to. (*Beat.*) At least you won't feel it. You won't remember it.

Jude begins to fall apart inside, but she pushes it down and remains cool. She just nods.

I'm scared, Jude.

Jude Me too. (*Beat.*) But we . . . We can take these bastards on. Yes we can. They think they know, oh how they think they know, and they're flyin' high as kites right now dreamin' on it. But they know nothing!

Acton Nothing!

Jude We're gonna flip this trampoline, Acton, take hold and turn their plan upside down, trick-or-treat-and-halloween 'em.

Acton Boo. Piece of candy!

Jude They think your pushover sister won't know, but it's them that won't know. We plan it right and it's us are gonna laugh so hard. At them! Fuckin' losers!

Acton laughs out loud.

Acton Oh yeah!

Acton starts making a list.

I'll make a list of what we have to do so nothing goes wrong . . . Should I ask Hoke for two pills to make sure you don't wake up?

Jude I'm not a cow, Acton. One pill is enough. But first I need you to promise me two things. One, no one can ever know. Not Mom, not anyone. Two. You gotta stay and watch.

Acton What? No way! I can't watch /

Jude (*cuts him off*) You got to. You have to make sure they don't. Hurt me. They've never done it before. They're virgins. Leave them alone, anything could happen.

Acton But Jude . . .

Jude I've got to know I'm not alone when it's happening.

63

Acton What if they won't let me be there?

Jude Tell them it's a deal-breaker.

Acton I don't want to watch. I've never even seen /

Jude You can look away. At the ceiling or play your guitar but you have to be there and keep me safe.

Acton is quiet some moments.

Acton Okay.

Jude Promise me.

Acton I promise.

Jude Pinkie promise.

After a moment they lock pinkies.

I want Frayne to go first.

Acton How come?

Jude 'Cause he'll be careful.

Acton Hoke wants to go first.

Jude Jesus. How many details did you talk about?

Acton just shrugs.

Look. Tell Frayne, when you get him by himself, that if I knew, you're sure I'd want him to go first. He likes me. He'll make it happen.

Acton He likes you a lot. He says you're really /

Jude Let's go inside and unpack your suitcase.

Jude lifts the suitcase and it's very heavy.

Acton I took the A-through-E encyclopedias.

Jude opens the suitcase.

You read those already so I didn't think you'd be too mad if I took them.

Jude picks up the 'A' book.

Jude Man, I loved 'A'. All those words you gotta say with an open mouth and it's always at the beginning. Look here: 'Aalen'.

Acton Aalen.

Jude A town in Germany. 'Aardwolf'. It feeds on decomposed animal substances, larvae and termites.

Acton You're saving me, Jude.

Jude Sure, but the coolest part of it is: they won't even know *we won this game*. Only you and I will know that we Topped Their Love. And we will! 'Cause nobody, nobody fucks –

Acton *and* **Jude** – with our kingdom.

Jude We stick –

Acton *and* **Jude** – together!

Acton You're the best sister in the whole / world.

Jude You want marshmallows in your chocolate milk or not?

Acton Not.

Jude Then come on inside.

Act Two

SCENE ONE

Jude, Hoke and Frayne. 1991. Diggs' bare porch. A half-hour later. At some point, Young Jude enters the basement, lies down and covers herself.

Hoke What?

Frayne Christ.

Hoke Acton told you what?

Frayne What did he say?

Jude (*calm*) In a nutshell? That you threatened him with certain death at the hands of his former tormentors unless he let you fuck me.

Frayne (*whispers*) Oh my God.

Hoke No. Your brother, he said. We agreed, we. No.

Jude Acton gave me the pill, I popped it, I passed out, you both tripped down to the basement and one by one you stuck it to me. All under fifteen minutes and all the while enveloped in the most enticing of pink clouds: *Jude will never know.* Well, I did. I knew.

Hoke and Frayne are dumbfounded.

Hoke Oh my God.

Jude (*triumphant*) Yep.

Frayne Jesus.

Jude Yep.

Hoke You knew?

Jude Yep.

Hoke You knew?

Jude Yep.

Hoke Please stop saying that.

Frayne When exactly did Acton tell you?

Hoke (*to Frayne*) Come on. She's lying.
  (*To Jude.*) I bet you didn't know till Acton told you.
Afterwards.

Jude My brother and I had no secrets.

Hoke I don't believe you. What kind of girl would. What
girl –

Jude – would agree to be drugged and then screwed by the
likes of you?

Hoke Exactly. No girl would.

Jude But I wasn't just any girl now, was I?

Hoke I still don't believe you'd /

Jude Take a fuckin' look at me. Who do you think I am?

*Hoke looks at her, then looks away. Jude speaks calmly
at first, but we see her youthful energy returning,
building inside her, invigorating her.*

(*Facts.*) Till just a few minutes ago, you were what? Two
bad boys, lickety-splits, ornery rascals with a reeky little
crime in your pocket? Tuck your fingers in and it still sticks
like candy, just a whiff of the crooked, the crummy, the *Oh
my God did we really do that when we were kids? If
anyone ever knew? But we were only kids and kids do crazy
things when their skin's on fire. Anything can happen,
anything can happen.* (*Beat.*) Sure I popped that pill that
night and I lay down in your mind like *a drunken, pretty
bitch, knocked out, flying high over teeter-totter land* and
you thought Acton'd sell me like a bag of onions, for what?

And all these years you been tootin' your horn in the dark, toot, toot, with that sharp little buzz still kickin': *We shouldn't've done it but we did it. We shouldn't've done it but we did it and most everybody else never did it like that so we're special, we're tailor-made.* Well. I got news for you: You didn't do anything *exceptional.* You didn't even break the law. And with Acton dead – and yes I blame you both for not keeping him alive as well as every tall building under construction that doesn't give a fuck who falls as long as they finish the job – I might as well claim it: Your boneheaded little contest? Yep. We won it! Me and my brother, we tricked your pony, my friends. Way back when, we flipped your scheme. W-T-Y-L. We Topped Your Love!

Silence some moments.

Hoke Wow.

Jude Yeah. Wow.

Hoke And here you were, pretending to be all offended when we said we'd only felt you up a little.

Jude I was amazed at how badly you lied.

Frayne We were trying to tell you a little part of the story.

Hoke Yeah, to relieve the pressure.

Jude Of your anxiety or your cock?

Hoke (*unfazed*) We told Acton he had to give up what he loved most. Well, that'd be you. But we were gonna accept the rat.

Jude Liar.

Frayne It's true.

Hoke But the next day here comes your brother: 'Okay. I'll give you my sister.' Well what the fuck! We were lean and hungry and we said –

Frayne (*quietly*) Rock me, baby.

68

Hoke Yeah we did. Can you blame us?

Jude You talked about the plan in detail with my brother.

Hoke We got off on talking about it. But we didn't think he'd go for it.

Frayne But we hoped.

Hoke No we did not. We didn't believe it could ever happen.

Frayne You didn't hope? Well, we sure didn't hesitate when Acton agreed.

Hoke The fuck we didn't. You started crying.

Frayne I did not.

Hoke Bullshit. You were bawling.

Frayne 'Cause you hit me in the gut when I tried to tell him it was a joke.

Hoke grabs Frayne's collar.

Hoke I hit you 'cause you were nothing but a punk, for all your mean, hard-as-nails I'll-bully-your-ass-to-Cambodia-and-back shit. You were scared as a baby bird, scared to step up and take hold of a possibility on a fucking plate and you're no different now, Frayne.

Hoke releases Frayne.

Frayne Right. Then let me rephrase that: *you* didn't hesitate.

Hoke Look here: we now know that Judith masterminded a non-crime. Jude set it up. Jude put it in motion.

Jude Stop saying my name.

Frayne You could have said 'no'.

Jude *You* could have said 'no'.

Hoke I've had years, years feeling bad about this.

69

Jude Mixed with some tangy thrill.

Hoke (*shrugs*) Some.

Jude How much guilt and regret?

Hoke Plenty.

Jude Music to my ears. And you?

Frayne Not a shit day goes by without you in it.

Jude I'm so glad.

Hoke And fear too. That someone would find out and it would.

Frayne Sure. That one day it'd bite us in the ass.

Jude Chomp, chomp. (*Beat.*) Guilt, regret, fear. Just what I'd hoped for.

Hoke Yeah. But now we're. Free. There was no mo-les-ta-tion. I mean, you can't steal from yourself and you can't abuse the willing, right?

Jude Acton is still dead.

Hoke Yes. As a doornail. And I loved that doornail even though I now know he pulled a hell of a lot of wood over –

Frayne (*interrupts*) Wool.

Hoke Yeah, over our eyes, but at least today we know Acton didn't kill himself because he thought we'd fucked /

Jude (*cuts him off*) – raped his sister.

Hoke 'Cause we didn't and he knew it.

Jude He never got over what happened that night.

Hoke Neither did I but I didn't jump off a bridge.

Jude You are kind of a masterpiece, you know it?

Hoke Museum quality, baby. This changes everything.

Frayne Does it? We thought we raped her.

Hoke But we didn't. We were oh-so-slyly duped.

Frayne But we had intent to commit a crime.

Jude Yes. You did.

Hoke Look. When it comes down to it, I'd say we, we are the ones who /

Jude Let me say it for you: are the victims?

Hoke I was going to say we're the ones who remember that night, not you. We're still fucked up about it. You're a blank.

Frayne You don't remember anything?

Jude How could I? I was out cold. I even woke up laughing.

Hoke You woke up laughing? Fucking hell . . . Just tell me this: don't you ever wish your brother had kept his damn mouth shut and just gone through with the plan? Then you'd never have known at all.

Jude But Acton would have known.

Hoke Yeah, and maybe found comfort in the fact that you didn't.

Jude It wasn't that big a deal: I was a slut.

Frayne No you were not.

Jude You think it was the first time a couple of boys fucked me when I was comatose?

Frayne Yes. I do.

Young Acton enters, carrying a heavy book. The 'A' encyclopedia. He begins to read, quietly, in the background. They do not see him.

Jude Look. What was left of our family, I had to keep it together. Isn't that what good girls do?

71

Acton Ague.

Hoke No good girl I ever met would go so far as to /

Jude Hoke. Stop.

Acton From Latin. A form or stage of malarial disease.

Jude If you continue to speculate on things you can never fathom, I will seek out your beautiful wife Carol, tonight even, and tell her and her two pin-headed offspring –

Acton The ague fit –

Jude About the origins of your sexual past.

Acton – is the cold, shivering stage . . .

Jude When I describe your half-crime, your oopsy-daisy-almost-crime, their jaws will drop.

Acton Alignment, used in drawing and in military arrangements.

Hoke Okay, Judith. Okay. Even though it's quite obvious to both Frayne and I that you were, as a young woman, and still are, warped, spiteful, and of unsound mind – all of which, by the way, can be treated with medication – I will suspend judgement.

Jude Thank you.

Acton Altar.

Hoke But come near my family and I will crush you like a beetle. Hell of a crack.

Acton A base or pedestal used for sacrifice to gods –

Jude I understand.

Acton – or to deified heroes.

Jude Family is sacrosanct.

Frayne If it's any consolation, it was over so quick I hardly knew what hit me.

Hoke I hit you. Again. 'Cause you wouldn't fuckin' hurry up. Acton gave us seven and a half minutes each and you were on your eighth.

Jude Did you cum?

Frayne No.

Acton Anatomy.

Jude (*to Hoke*) You?

Acton To cut up.

Hoke (*nods 'yes'*) With two minutes left to go.

Acton Cutting asunder.

Frayne Well, I'm sorry and I regret it every day of my life.

Jude turns away from him.

Years later when I began to sleep with women, I didn't feel. Much. There was this girl /

Hoke Oh come on, bud. Don't do this.

Frayne Wild like a thistle, take-no-prisoners beautiful /

Hoke Have some self-respect.

Acton Architecture.

Frayne Cynthia.

Hoke I remember her.

Frayne But I couldn't. *Want* her.

Acton The art of building in such a way –

Frayne Really want her, though I wanted to.

Acton – as to accord with principles determined.

73

Frayne One night she gets drunk and I can't wake her up and then suddenly I'm so /

Hoke Jesus, Frayne.

Frayne I feel like my body's gonna rip me apart.

Jude So let me guess: you fucked her when she was passed out?

Frayne I felt.

Acton Aureola.

Frayne It felt.

Acton The radiance of luminous cloud.

Frayne Like a switch went on in a room that'd been dark for years. And I. I /

Hoke Okay, that's enough. But thank you for that piece of emotional whatever, Frayne.

Acton Auscultation. An act of listening . . .

Jude Did you do your best after that to get your pretty little thistle drunk as a skunk as often as you could?

Frayne Something like that.

Hoke Me, I'm a bull. I've been with Carol thirteen years and she still gets me hot. Every step she takes. And I like it when she's wide awake, Frayne. Lights on. Hello, hello. And she likes it too.

Frayne (*to Jude*) There's one thing you might not know about that night.

Hoke Frayne. Can we please quit now?

Frayne You may have been out cold that night, but you were. Wet. When I /

74

Hoke Jesus, shut the fuck up!

Frayne When I was /

Hoke (*nears him*) If you don't stop I will hit you like I never have before.

Jude Hoke. It's okay.
(*To Frayne.*) Go on.

Frayne When I was inside you, you became /

Jude (*cuts him off*) Wet. Yes, I heard that part.

Frayne How do you account for that?

Jude Meat sweats in the open air?

Young Acton now sits beside Young Jude, who is still asleep, and reads to her.

Acton Austin.

Frayne You were not meat.

Hoke Oh my.

Jude The body's a strange place. Even when its light's out, it's tumblin' in the dark.

Hoke Enough, okay. We can read that night any way we want. Me? Of course I'm sorry. It was fucked up and nothing was ever the same after that. And if it's any consolation, and this is, of course, something I would never ever want Carol to know . . .

Acton Built on high bluffs –

Hoke You were the hottest girl I ever had.

Acton – one hundred and twenty feet above the river –

Hoke And the first girl.

Acton – which is spanned by a bridge.

Hoke I know it sounds kind of twisted and there's an element of poor timing here, but I want to thank you for that. So: thank you, Jude.

After a moment, Jude laughs briefly. Hoke grins. Jude composes herself.

Jude (*quietly*) You're welcome.

SCENE TWO

Acton is sitting in the half-dark, reading to Jude from the 'A' encyclopedia. Jude is still asleep. Acton will use his inhaler three or four times during the scene.

Acton Austin. Austin was first settled in 1838 and was named Waterloo. But a year later it was renamed in honor of Stephen F. –

Suddenly Jude is awake.

Jude *and* **Acton** – Austin.

Jude Austin?

Acton Yeah. One of its founders!

Jude looks around disorientated.

Jude It didn't work, Acton. The pill didn't work!

Acton You okay?

Jude What happened? It didn't work!

Acton Shhhhh.

Jude I've only been out a couple of secs.

Acton Longer than that.

Jude No way. I hardly closed my eyes. I /

Acton Jude. You were asleep. Deep asleep.

Jude I was?

Acton For three hours.

Jude Oh. I thought.

Acton Does your head hurt?

Jude No. My mouth's a little dry. (*Beat.*) So it. Worked?

Acton Yeah.

Jude And they're.

Acton Gone. Left a couple hours ago.

Jude How long were.

Acton Fifteen minutes, like we said. Quick.

After a moment:

Jude Good.

Acton Fourteen, actually.

Jude Fourteen?

Acton To be exact. Quick.

Jude I woke up so fast I thought maybe.

Acton I've been here all this time.

Jude Seems like only a few seconds.

Acton That's how the pill works.
(*Giggles.*) You farted before you woke up.

Jude I did? (*Beat.*) But not when. When they were.

Acton Oh no. No. Long after they. (*Beat.*) I got your PJs ready right here, like you said.

Jude But it went. Okay?

Acton Okay and quick.

Jude What else?

Acton Nothing else. Simple. Just one, two, three.

Jude But it was only Hoke and Frayne, not three /

Acton Oh no. No! I just meant one, two, three and it was done. And Frayne went first, like you /

Jude They didn't do anything else to me /

Acton Just what we. Agreed.

Jude Did they try?

Acton No way. They stuck to the rules. Hoke was shaking so bad I thought he'd fall down, what a scaredy-cat. I never figured him for a /

Jude (*cuts him off*) But they both.

Acton Yeah. But, quick.

Jude Stop saying that word.

A moment of silence.

Acton Are you okay?

Jude I think so. I don't hurt.

Acton I would never let them hurt /

Jude Something's a bit different but.

Acton What? What, Jude?

Jude briefly feels between her legs.

Jude Maybe it's just. A little sore. Sticky. (*Beat.*) But they used /

Acton Yes they did. I watched them put them on. One on. One on each.

Jude Nothing tore?

Acton I checked after. I filled them both with water from the tap and there were no leaks. But.

Jude But what?

Acton can't say it. Jude begins to panic.

But what, Acton? Tell me.

Acton There was some.

Jude (*afraid*) Acton! Just say it. What else did they do – ?

Acton (*quickly*) Nothing! There was just some. Blood.

Jude (*relieved*) Oh.

Acton But only a bit. On Frayne's – . I know it was his 'cause his was see-through and Hoke's was blue.

Jude Blue?

Acton He said it was glow-in-the-dark but it didn't really.
(*Rushed.*) I swear I made them do everything right, Jude, and I watched over them like a hawk, I promise. Are you hurt, please don't be hurt?

Jude I'm not hurt, Acton. It's normal. There's little blood when it's a first time.

Acton But it wasn't your first. You had Richard. Richard at the Wet and Wild! And two others, you said you.

Jude is silent a moment.

Jude And Mom?

Acton Mom got back from her late shift and came down a minute to say goodnight and happy birthday again and to ask about the party and I told her it was a big success and that you were worn out, fast asleep. She kissed you right –

Acton touches Jude's forehead to demonstrate. Jude involuntarily flinches.

– there.

Acton takes a tiny, wrapped box from his pocket and holds it out to Jude.

Happy birthday, Jude.

Jude just looks at the box but doesn't take it.

Jude I told Mom not to buy me a present.

Acton Open it. She was kind of excited about it. I could tell.

Acton shakes the little box next to his ear to tempt Jude.

Jude I got to shower first.

Jude stands up.

Acton Wait, Jude! You're not –

Jude now realizes she's naked from the waist down.

Jude (*facts*) Oh, right. Forgot. Hand me my PJs.

Acton does. Jude slips them on. Then leaves.

SCENE THREE

A half-hour later. 1991. Jude, Frayne and Hoke make a toast. After the toast, no one drinks again.

Hoke As fucked up and fucked over as we were, are, may we hope for some reconcilia— /

Jude May we find sleep.

Hoke (*concedes*) May we find sleep.

Frayne May we find wakeful women in our beds.

They all laugh and drink.

And may Acton be at peace.

All May Acton be at peace.

Hoke I could never jump off a bridge. I'd take an overdose.

Frayne The kid always had flair.

Jude (*to Frayne*) And you? How would you do it?

Frayne Oh. Gun. That way I'd be sure. You?

Jude Jump. From somewhere high.

Hoke Like brother like sis— /

Jude (*cuts him off*) But not traffic. Water. I'd jump into fast, deep water. From way high up.

Hoke Whoa.

Jude Sometimes I wonder, if I'd come home /

Hoke Don't, Jude. Acton was a softie. He wasn't like the rest of us.

Jude You think?

Hoke Sure. Maybe he was spared the worst of it, but he still couldn't /

Jude My brother was spared nothing.

Frayne He means at least Acton didn't have to watch.

Hoke What we did.

Jude What do you mean?

Hoke I mean at least he didn't see us do it. To you.

Jude Acton saw all of it.

Frayne He wasn't in the room.

Jude Of course he was in the room. My brother was in the room the whole time.

Hoke Uh, no he wasn't.

Frayne Acton stood outside the door, timing us. One thousand. Two thousand.

Hoke I had to keep telling him to shut up.

Jude He watched your every move.

Hoke Hey. We might have been perverts, but we were not so sick as to make your brother watch /

Jude Acton was there in the basement with me the whole time.

Frayne Why do you keep saying that?! Acton stood outside the door, halfway up the stairs, keeping watch and counting.

Hoke And at every minute he'd shout 'Twelve minutes to go . . . Eleven minutes to go.' It was a miracle we could 'go' at all.

Jude Acton swore to me.

Frayne Then he lied to you.

Jude No. We had a deal: I would do it if he would stay and be my. Witness.

Hoke Witness?

Jude To. To make sure nothing. To make sure you didn't hurt me.

Frayne We didn't hurt you, Jude.

Hoke Course not. What kind of scum do you /

Jude (*cuts him off*) My brother watched you put on your condoms.

Hoke True. And then he left.

Jude Why are you lying to me?!

Frayne Jude.

Jude (*shouts*) Why are you lying?!

Hoke Calm down, Jesus! So your brother couldn't bear to watch his two best friends . . . The poor kid was shaking like a leaf. He could hardly breathe.

Jude We promised each other. That he . . . That he'd watch everything that happened that night.

Frayne Nothing happened that night but what. Happened. What we agreed.

Jude cannot speak for a moment.

Jude How can I. But then how can I know for sure that.

Hoke He was right outside the door. We knew the limits. We'd made a deal.

Jude But if Acton wasn't there then you could have made me. Kiss you or. Or.

Hoke We didn't kiss you. You were out cold.

Jude Or use other things besides. In me. Put things in me. People do that.

Hoke Not people like us.

Jude Yes, people like you!

Frayne No, that's not what /

Jude They stick things in, they laugh –

Hoke No one laughed at –

Jude They touch you how they're not supposed to, in places /

83

Hoke Shut the hell up, Jude!

Jude They do things they normally wouldn't and /

Hoke (*shouts*) Nothing like that happened!

Silence some moments.

Frayne (*quietly*) I promise: nothing like that happened.

Hoke Oh Jesus Christ, can we let this be over? Please, please can we just let this be over? Look, I've got to get up early for a flight tomorrow to –

Hoke *and* **Frayne** Atlanta.

Frayne Sure. We know.

Hoke And it's movie night with the kids. Popcorn, Twizzlers.

Jude My Linda loves Twizzlers.

Hoke Which flavor?

Hoke *and* **Jude** Strawberry flavor.

Jude Yeah. Linda and I always take a pack of them with us when we go up to Barton Springs. It's a natural spring and we like to go in winter when the water's so hot it takes your breath away. If we get there real early, it's no one else but us so we strip and jump. Linda always shrieks like a train. When we climb out, our bodies are steaming and we're like two ghosts dissolving in the air.

Frayne Huh. That sounds nice.

Jude It is.

Hoke (*to Frayne*) You still coming by Sunday for roast?
    (*To Jude.*) You're welcome too. Anytime. I'd like you to meet the kids.

Jude just nods.

Frayne Not this time.

Hoke Huh?

Frayne Tell Carol I'm sorry but I won't be able to make it this time.

Hoke Frayne. You think I don't know you won't ever be round for Sunday roast again? Yeah. I know it. But what you didn't know back then was that I didn't really give a shit about failing my SATs.

Frayne Yes you did.

Hoke Not really. Hide what you love, right? Top of the list was always my Firebird.

Frayne shakes his head in disbelief.

At high speed hovering like ice on water. And in that gap in between, that kid Hoke thought he was something else than what he was. Mostly I loved that car 'cause it was the only place where the four of us could pack in tight together. And we were all, just for a few minutes, moving in the same direction.

(*To Jude.*) You only rode with us once. I gave you –

Jude – a ride to work, yeah.

Hoke You never rode with me again. Said I was reckless.

Jude *and* **Frayne** You were.

Hoke But you know what the fuck of it all is? I love my wife Carol. I love my kids. When I look at them at the most banal of moments and there's a smear of spaghetti sauce on a cheek and I lick my finger to wipe it off and my heart just jerks like it's going to vacate my body. You know what that's like, Jude?

Jude Sure. I know.

Hoke But I. Can't get past this feeling at the same time that Carol and the kids are cover for something I love more. More than them. That my love for them is a decoy. It's impossible, of course, because I got nothing, nothing else that matters to me so help me God that I love more but it's always there, the doubt, the counterfeit and no matter how hard I try, it stays.

Frayne (*coldly*) Take a pill for it, Hoke.

Hoke (*nods*) But then I might not know what I know I feel – and the thought that I wouldn't and that whatever it is would just go on without my knowing it's there inside me is –

> *Hoke breaks off, nods goodbye and leaves, just as Young Jude enters. She puts on the coat of her older self and gets ready to leave.*

SCENE FOUR

Diggs' porch. 1977. Six weeks later. Jude is wearing what might be her father's coat. Dawn, cold. The old suitcase is packed. Acton is in his PJs and slippers.

Acton That's Dad's coat.

Jude I filled the freezer with chicken and burgers. Froze some vegetables too. You'll have enough for a month.

Acton It's way too big for you.

Jude There's a jar with bills behind the stove but only for emergencies. Just enough to turn the electric on if it goes out.

Acton This will kill Mom.

Jude Mom will be fine.

Acton What should I tell her?

Jude That Grandma needs me. I'll send money when I get a job.

Acton I know what it is, Jude: you hate me.

Jude You're my brother.

Acton You hate your brother.

Jude When I see the two of them, I want to –

Acton Puke. Yeah, me too.

Jude – laugh. I want to laugh so hard I'll choke. They think they stole something from us but they didn't. They slink around me like thieves, scared to death. They think they got a deep, dark secret but the secret is mine. Mine! Only I can't tell it so I got to leave.

Acton takes this in.

Acton A few weeks ago a kid whacked me on the head with a book in science class. So I picked up a dissected frog, popped it in my mouth and chewed it like a cracker. Didn't even gag. One boy fainted. No one bothers me anymore and it's got nothing to do with Frayne or Hoke. I wish I'd eaten a frog a long time ago. (*Beat.*) In a few years Hoke is gonna get me a good job with Health First. He says his dad can pull a string for college too.

Jude You got straight A's. You don't need a string.

Acton Straight A's aren't enough and you know it. I want opportunity.

Jude Always hated that word: *opportunity*. Come to think of it, there's nothing in this world I care about that begins with 'O'. I'm seventeen. I wash dishes at the Melrose Inn at night. My hands are already old. Opportunity?

Jude turns to leave.

Acton If you love me, Jude, you . . . Please don't leave me.

Without warning, Jude tackles Acton.

Jude (*explodes*) You could've said, *I won't let you do it, I won't let you do it, you're my sister. You're my sister! I won't, I won't, I won't.*

After her outburst, Jude gets off of Acton. All fight suddenly drained from them both.

(*Steady.*) You could have said. *No.*

Jude gets up. Acton sits up, but stays where he is. Jude speaks without looking at Acton.

The old tractor tire in the yard Dad strung up in a tree by a chain? We'd hold on to it, you and me, upside down, to see who could last the longest. We'd count, one thousand, two thousand –

Acton gets up.

Acton – yeah, three thousand, four thousand.

Acton continues to count, quietly under his breath.

Jude The blood pouring into our heads till we were drunk with it.

Acton Nine thousand, ten thousand.

Jude Close your eyes. Don't watch me leave.

Acton does, and Jude turns him around so he's not facing her. Acton keeps counting, almost inaudible.

I can still see us, swinging on that tire. Our legs are upside down, our hair is upside down, our eyes. All of us, upside down but everything was right.

Jude picks up the suitcase and leaves.

1991. Some minutes later. Jude comes down to the basement alone.
  After some moments Frayne comes down to the basement.

Frayne You can use my truck, Jude. For however long you /

Jude *(cuts him off)* Thought you left. I don't need your truck.

Frayne I want you to have it.

Jude Soon as I pack up here, empty the house, I'm back to Austin. Back to my daughter Linda. Maybe Linda will show me how to do it different this time.

Frayne Why don't you come on home, Jude? You and your daughter, you could /

Jude *(calmly interrupts)* You say you're sorry. Be sorry. What happened in those fourteen minutes? Exactly.

Frayne Judith.

Jude So you and Hoke come down to the basement. And there I am.

  She waits.

And there I am.

  Finally Frayne relents.

Frayne Out cold.

Jude You put on the condoms.

Frayne First we.

Jude Undress, of course. And you take off her pants. What's the color of her underwear?

  Frayne hears the use of the third person but continues. Jude doesn't seem to notice the slip.

Frayne She isn't wearing any.

Jude That's right. To make it easier, quicker.

Frayne Her boots are already off. Hoke wants to take her socks off but I stop him.

Jude True. She wakes up later with her socks on. What can you see in the dark?

Frayne Almost nothing. Just a glow of skin. We put the condoms on, which is hard because we aren't . . . But finally we get them on.

Jude That's when my brother leaves her alone with the two of you.

Frayne Acton can hardly stand he's so scared. He says, 'Don't hurt me.'

Jude You mean he says, 'Don't hurt her.'

Frayne No. He says, 'Don't hurt me.' He's confused. He leaves the room. I go first. Then Hoke. Then it's over. There is nothing else. There was nothing else. I promise you that.

Jude nods, wanting to believe him.

Afterwards, Acton comes back in and he says, 'I'm cold,' and covers her up. But it's your skin that's cold. Acton says /

Jude (*cuts him off*) That's enough.

Frayne Acton says, 'I'm still asleep,' but he's awake. You're the one who's asleep. He /

Jude (*firm*) Stop it. Just. Stop.

Quiet between them.

We were so young that night.

Frayne Yeah.

Jude So young there's nothing in the world but what we can see right in front of us. And we've no idea of the size of the thing barreling towards us, the incomprehensible momentum of it.

Frayne It's a fucking pile-up.

Jude And I'm thinking: *I can make this thing work the way we need it to. I can save everyone I love. I can forge us a life where we're not afraid, where we have work and a roof and the lights are on, if only I . . . If only I can just hold my hands in the fire a little longer and command that heat.*

Frayne Jude. No one can do that alone.

Jude Yeah. But when you're seventeen you think you're making this life but really it's making you, and then you.

Jude stops suddenly. No longer wanting to share her thoughts with Frayne.

I got to get started here, pack things up.

Frayne Would you like some help?

Jude No.

Frayne I want to ask.

Jude drops the truck keys back in Frayne's hand. She waits.

Jude Ask.

Frayne Before that night, Acton told me you were gonna kiss me on your birthday. I didn't believe it. Was it true?

Jude Yes.

They are quiet a moment.

Frayne I still want to kiss you.

Jude (*no emotion*) Go to hell.

Frayne nods.

Frayne I just needed to say that. Goodbye, Jude.

Frayne turns to leave.

Jude Frayne. I did kiss you that night. Don't you remember? In that other world. The one we didn't choose.

Frayne disappears.

SCENE SIX

Jude is by herself in the basement. 1991. For the first time, she sits.

Now Young Jude and Young Acton appear from 1977. And this time Jude can see them.

Jude is imagining a version of the past that didn't happen, but could have.

Young Jude You made that up!

Acton Nope. Found it in the P's. Pogonip! It means a cold fog full of frozen particles . . .

Young Jude snatches a rolled streamer from Acton's hands.

Young Jude You're not supposed to jump ahead. You got to read the books in order.

Without looking at her, Acton throws the streamer to Jude, who catches it.

Acton I'm gonna read them backwards: Pogonip.

Young Jude I like the sound of it.

Acton Hoke and Frayne are gonna beat the shit out of me tonight when I tell 'em I won't give them my sister.

Young Jude Look, if I give them both a big fat tongue kiss tonight, they'll forget all about it.

Acton I hope you're right.

Young Jude I'm always right.

Acton Thanks, Jude.

Young Jude You'll find better friends –

Acton – when we move to Florida.

Young Jude Yeah! Sunshine State here we come!

Acton And Mom can get some heat on her bones! And Skimpy can meet Grandma, and warm her tumors in the sun.

Jude *and* **Young Jude** Acton.

Acton hears his name but he's not sure who called it.

Acton Huh?

Young Jude What are we gonna say to Hoke and Frayne?

Young Jude *and* **Acton** No *fucking way!*

Acton 'Cause Jude and Acton stick together! Top that!

Jude *and* **Acton** Top Our Love!

Acton We Diggs are kinda kick-ass, aren't we?

Young Jude Yeah we are! Just wish Dad were here for my birthday. I miss him.

Acton I miss his arm.

Quiet. Then they both burst out laughing. Then Young Jude launches into their game.

Young Jude So Dad's falling from the fourteenth floor, head first towards the pavement:

Acton *I didn't even get to eat my lunch and my wife's packed my favorite salami!*

Young Jude Dad's thinkin': *That damn boy of mine better win the science fair this summer!*

Acton *He won it last year! I bet he wins it this year too!* Dad's thinking:

Young Jude *My kids are gettin' off the school bus right now and they've no idea I'm fallin'. Yellow bus –*

Acton *Yellow sun on my back.*

Young Jude *It's middle of the day and –*

Acton *– I'm fallin' fast but I won't close my eyes!*

Young Jude *I'm wide awake!*

Jude And he's thinking:

Acton (*loud*) *I want to live!*

> *Acton jumps up on a raised level at the back of the stage, playing the game. His back is to us. We could be anywhere.*

Young Jude *I want to live but I'm fallin'!*

Jude *You're falling.*

Acton *Can you see me?!*

Jude *and* **Young Jude** Yes.

Acton *Can they see me – ?*

Young Jude *I can see you!*

Jude *You're not alone.*

Young Jude *Bye, bye, birdie!*

Acton *Catch me!*

> *Jude stands up.*

Jude *and* **Young Jude** *I'll catch you!*

> *Acton raises his arms in celebration.*

Young Jude *and* **Acton** *I'm here! I'm falling!*

All Catch me.

> *Acton jumps just as lights go out.*
> *End of play.*